Anne Frank

Women of War - Book 6
History Nerds

Table of Contents

Introduction

How can words scribbled by candlelight in a cramped attic transcend space, time, and the worst human atrocities? How can they ignite hope in the hearts of millions? As we discover Anne Frank's diary, we ponder this profound question. It lies at the heart of understanding the diary's enduring impact and the seeds of hope it planted amidst the darkness of the Holocaust.

To grasp the significance, we must first consider the context in which Anne wrote her diary. She filled its pages during a time when war, hatred, and unimaginable cruelty engulfed the world. The Frank family, along with millions of other Jews, hid from being discovered and sent to concentration camps. Each day they lived in constant fear. In this atmosphere of terror and despair, Anne's diary stood as a defiant act of hope and humanity.

For years after the war, the power of Anne's words remained largely unknown. Her intimate thoughts as a young girl grappling with adolescence against unfathomable evil nearly became lost to history. Only through chance events and dedication did those who recognized the diary's potential ensure Anne's voice was finally heard.

Many might assume the diary's impact was immediate and inevitable - that its wisdom and poignancy would be instantly recognized. But the reality is far more complex. In the war's aftermath, as survivors rebuilt lives and nations moved forward, painful memories were often pushed aside. The idea that a teenage girl's diary could hold profound truths for humanity may have seemed far-fetched.

What sets Anne's story apart is the tireless efforts of those refusing to let her words fade into obscurity. From Miep Gies preserving the diary pages after the family's arrest, to Anne's father Otto editing and publishing the diary, to countless translators, publishers, and educators bringing her story worldwide - each role was crucial in ensuring Anne's voice was heard.

Today, Anne Frank's diary has transformed how we understand and remember the Holocaust. Through Anne's eyes, we see human faces and dreams, not just statistics and facts. We are reminded of the indomitable human spirit's power to shine through even darkness. The diary has inspired plays, films, and art worldwide, selling over 30 million copies in 70+ languages.

Some may argue focusing on one girl's story risks oversimplifying or romanticizing the Holocaust. Others question whether Anne's diary, with its youthful perspective, truly captures the full horror. These are valid concerns addressed head-on. Ultimately, though, Anne's diary offers a personal, human glimpse into a world defying easy comprehension.

As we journey into Anne's world, let us carry these lessons. Let us remember hope can be found in unexpected places, and the smallest voices can echo through eternity. Most of all, let us honor her legacy by working to build a world where such atrocities never happen again. For this is perhaps the most fitting tribute to the girl who dared dream, hope, and believe in fundamental human goodness, even as the world descended into unthinkable darkness.

Who were the Franks?

The Frank family's life before the war was a tapestry woven with threads of comfort, love, and the everyday moments that define a family. It began in Frankfurt, Germany, a city they called home until the dark clouds of Nazism loomed on the horizon.

Anne Frank was born into a world where the promise of prosperity and stability seemed unshakeable. Her parents, Otto Frank and Edith Frank-Holländer, provided a nurturing environment for Anne and her older sister, Margot. Otto was a dedicated businessman, managing his family's bank and later branching out to start his own company. Edith, hailing from a wealthy family, brought warmth and tradition into their household.

The Franks were an assimilated Jewish family, deeply rooted in both their heritage and their German identity. They celebrated Jewish holidays and customs, yet were equally integrated into the fabric of German society. Anne and Margot enjoyed a typical childhood, filled with the joys of learning, play, and friendship.

However, in 1933, the rise of Adolf Hitler and the Nazi Party marked the beginning of a new and terrifying chapter for Jews in Germany. Otto, ever the pragmatic and protective father, decided to seek refuge for his family in a safer place. He moved to Amsterdam in 1933, establishing the groundwork for a new life, while Edith, Anne, and Margot followed him in 1934.

Amsterdam, with its canals and vibrant culture, became their new home. Otto Frank's entrepreneurial spirit led him to set up a company called Opekta, which specialized in selling pectin for making jam. This venture provided the Franks with a stable income and the means to rebuild their lives.

In Amsterdam, the Franks found a welcoming community and a sense of normalcy. They settled in a pleasant neighborhood, where Anne and Margot attended school and quickly made new friends. Anne, with her lively spirit and inquisitive mind, thrived at the Montessori School. Margot, more reserved but equally bright, excelled in her studies.

The Frank family's life in Amsterdam was marked by the rhythms of daily life. Edith managed the household with care, ensuring that her daughters had a loving and nurturing environment. Otto's business flourished, and the family enjoyed cultural activities and the beauty of their new city.

Despite being far from their original home, the Franks maintained their Jewish traditions while embracing the Dutch culture. They were part of the Jewish community in Amsterdam, finding solidarity and support among fellow refugees and long-time residents alike.

But the tranquility of their new life was shattered in May 1940 when Nazi Germany invaded the Netherlands. The occupation brought with it the harsh and oppressive anti-Jewish laws that the Franks had fled Germany to escape. Each passing day brought new restrictions and dangers.

Jewish children were expelled from general schools, forcing Anne and Margot to attend the Jewish Lyceum. Social and economic freedoms were stripped away, and the shadow of persecution grew ever darker.

Before the war, the Franks had been a close-knit family enjoying the simple pleasures of pre-war Europe. Their move to Amsterdam had provided a brief respite from the horrors of Nazi rule in Germany. Otto's foresight had bought them time, but the relentless spread of Nazi tyranny soon caught up with them.

As the world around them changed irrevocably, the Frank family faced the growing threat with a mixture of fear and resilience. Their story, before the shadows fell, was one of hope, adaptation, and the unbreakable bonds of family. Little did they know that their greatest challenge was yet to come, one that would test their strength and unity in ways they could never have imagined.

Chapter 1: Anne, the Annex, and the Diary

The Secret Annex at 263 Prinsengracht in Amsterdam seems an unlikely setting for an extraordinary tale. Yet within these confined quarters, eight Jews hid for two years during the Nazi occupation of the Netherlands in World War II. Among them was Anne Frank, a vibrant adolescent girl whose diary became one of the most poignant and widely-read accounts of the Holocaust.

From July 6, 1942 until their tragic discovery on August 4, 1944, the Annex residents lived in constant fear, boredom, tension and surprising normalcy. The occupants included the Frank family - Otto, Edith, Margot and Anne; the van Pels family - Hermann, Auguste and Peter; and Fritz Pfeffer, a dentist friend. They resided in a hidden apartment concealed behind a movable bookcase in Otto's office building. Miep Gies, Victor Kugler, Johannes Kleiman and Bep Voskuijl dedicated themselves to sustaining the residents.

The central challenge was maintaining humanity and sanity amidst isolation, confinement, and the threat of discovery. The close quarters led to conflicts and clashes. Anne wrote, "We're much too close together, and we get on each other's nerves." Tempers flared frequently due to food shortages, a demanding bathroom schedule, and the stress of their precarious situation.

Yet they strove to maintain structure and normalcy. Strict noise rules avoided detection by warehouse workers below. They scheduled meals, chores and studies, with the children continuing education through correspondence. Creativity became a lifeline, with Anne and Margot writing stories, and the families staging plays and celebrating holidays.

The emotional nucleus was Anne herself, maturing from a restless 13-year-old into a thoughtful young woman. Her diary, started as an autograph book on her birthday, became her trusted confidant for hopes, fears, and keen observations. Through writing, we see Anne grappling with identity, family conflict, and her dreams against the backdrop of genocide.

Anne's candid entries vividly paint the Annex experience - celebrating improvised Hanukkah gifts; rejoicing over dashed hopes of an Allied invasion; sharing a tentative first kiss with Peter; and wrestling with raging hormones and strained parental relations. Yet she never lost faith in life's beauty and people's goodness, writing, "I don't think of misery, but of remaining beauty," and "Where there's hope, there's life...it makes us strong again."

Their story's outcome was ultimately tragic, with discovery leading to deportation to concentration camps. Only Otto Frank survived. Yet revealed through Anne's diary, their story stands as an extraordinary example of resilience amidst unimaginable adversity. They demonstrated the human spirit can soar even in suffocating circumstances, finding meaning, love and joy.

Published after the war, Anne's diary became one of the world's most widely read books, translated into over 70 languages. More than a historical document, it testifies to the power of the human spirit and calls for action against bigotry and hate. As Anne wrote, "What is done cannot be undone, but one can prevent it happening again." Her words inspire new generations to build equality, compassion and respect.

The Annex residents, especially Anne, embodied hope's life-sustaining power and the refusal to surrender humanity in the face of oppression. Through vivid details of their lives, struggles and unexpected joys, Anne's diary puts a human face on the Holocaust. Yet it prompts reflection: Why did Anne's story capture the world's heart while millions remain unknown? How can we honor her legacy through action against injustice today? Anne dreamed of her diary being read long after the war as a testament to the human spirit's strength. Our challenge is transforming her words into a living legacy of resilience, hope and courage to resist hatred. As Anne wisely wrote, "How wonderful that nobody need wait to improve the world."

Anne Vs. The World

Anne Frank's diary offers an intimate look at her life in hiding during the Holocaust. When we compare her experiences to other Jewish children of that time, we see striking similarities and profound differences.

Anne's story embodies the shared suffering, fear, and resilience of Jewish youth persecuted by the Nazis. Yet her diary provides an unparalleled window into the mind of a young girl navigating adolescence amidst genocide.

To grasp the significance of this comparison, we must understand the common threads tying Anne's story to those of other Jewish children. Like Anne, countless youth saw their worlds shattered by the rise of Nazism. They faced ostracization, forced to wear yellow stars, and barred from schools and public spaces. Ultimately, they were torn from homes and families.

Whether hiding in attics, forests, ghettos, or enduring concentration camps' unimaginable horrors, these children fought daily for survival against starvation, disease, violence, and death. Anne's fears of discovery, longing for freedom, and grappling with identity mirrored experiences echoed by many

Holocaust survivors. Like others, she found solace in family, friendship, imagination, creativity, and hope.

Yet Anne's diary offers something exceptional - a vivid, real-time record of life under Nazi oppression. Most survivors told their stories retrospectively, shaped by time and knowing the war's outcome. In contrast, Anne's diary captures unfolding events with raw authenticity.

Through her words, we witness Nazi persecution's suffocating constriction. We feel hiding's tension and tedium – petty squabbles and profound fears intermingled with unexpected joys and crushing despairs. We watch Anne grapple with universal adolescent challenges against unfathomable evil as her backdrop. Her diary humanizes the Holocaust's victims as individuals with dreams, quirks, and inner lives.

Moreover, Anne's forced confinement gives her diary a unique perspective. While other Jewish children fought for physical survival amid displacement and loss, Anne's battle was largely psychological. Trapped in the annex, she turned inward. Writing became her lifeline to preserve sanity and self. Her diary became a space for self-reflection and self-assertion - a way to transcend imprisoning walls.

This doesn't minimize other children's suffering, many enduring unimaginable physical and psychological torments. But it shows Anne's diary provides a lens into the Holocaust's impact on young minds and spirits. Her introspection, thirst for knowledge, and wisdom beyond her years make her story stand out as a testament to the resilience of the human spirit in darkness.

Yet Anne's uniqueness poses uncomfortable questions. Why has her diary become among the most widely-read Holocaust accounts while so many other stories remain untold? Is it her powerful writing, her relatable voice, or the diary's publication timing? Or does her narrative's humanity and hope make it more palatable than unrelenting horror faced by others?

These complex questions speak to the politics of Holocaust memory and representation. In elevating Anne's story, we mustn't erase or overshadow experiences of millions of silenced children. For every Anne Frank, countless others left no record - their stories lost to history. But this doesn't diminish her diary's value; it makes her words more precious, witnessing both her life and lives lost.

Ultimately, Anne's diary's power lies in bridging past and present, making the Holocaust feel not just historical but an intimate human tragedy. Her timeless words resonate themes of identity, connection, resisting injustice, and hope persisting despite despair.

In our world still grappling with the Holocaust's legacy, Anne's diary remains vital - a call to remember, empathize, and remain vigilant against hatred. By comparing her story to other children's, we honor the tragedy's enormity while also recognizing the individual voice's power to touch hearts across generations.

As we honor Anne's memory, let's also honor the lost stories. Let's strive for a world where no child faces the horrors she endured, where diversity celebrates, and rights protect. For Anne's diary isn't just past record, but a present and future call to action – a reminder that even in darkest times, the human spirit shines, offering generations hope and light.

So let's read Anne's words and remember. Let's learn from the resilience and sacrifice of her story and others'. And let's carry that legacy forward, working towards a world of safety, dignity and peace for all children.

Diary of a Young Girl Decoded

Anne Frank's diary continues to resonate deeply because it captures universal human experiences - love, fear, hope, and struggle against unimaginable darkness. Her words, penned while hiding as a Jewish teenager during the Holocaust, transcend her individual story to become a testament to the human spirit.

One powerful aspect is Anne's unwavering sense of identity. Despite being confined and stripped of freedom, she refused to let her circumstances define her. She wrote, "I don't want to have lived in vain. I want to be useful or bring enjoyment to all people, even those I've never met. I want to go on living even after my death!" This determination to matter and leave a mark is a desire readers viscerally connect with.

Anne's diary is also a masterclass in emotional honesty. She explored the full spectrum - joy, infatuation, fear, loneliness, despair. In one entry, she admitted, "I hardly care whether I live or die... I can't change events anyway." This raw vulnerability both heartbreaks and validates readers who faced their own dark nights.

Yet even in her lowest moments, Anne returned to hope. She wrote, "I still believe, in spite of everything, that people are truly good at heart." This ability to hold faith in humanity amidst atrocities is the essence of resilience. Readers draw strength from her indomitable spirit.

Anne also humanized an overwhelming tragedy. The Holocaust's scale can feel incomprehensible - just statistics numbing the mind. But Anne put a face to one of those six million Jewish lives lost. She wrote candidly about daily frustrations, budding romance, dreams for the future - reminding us the perished were rich individuals, not numbers.

Anne's diary powerfully shows writing's crucial role in resistance. By chronicling her experiences, she defied Nazi attempts to erase her existence, creating a permanent record that can never be silenced. For oppressed peoples everywhere, her example galvanizes: even when denied physical freedom, our minds and souls remain our own. No force can stop us documenting our truth. The diary is an eternal beacon inspiring the oppressed to keep telling stories.

On a craft level, Anne's writing is extraordinary for her youth. She had a novelist's gift for capturing senses and bringing characters to vivid life. Her philosophical musings belie profound wisdom. As she revised her diary for posterity, elevating her prose and pondering universal themes, it gained immediacy and timeless relevance.

Ultimately, Anne's diary miraculously fuses dark and light. In history's darkest chapter, this young girl found reason for faith and optimism. Imprisoned by hatred, she discovered within an "intense longing for everything beautiful and good." Subjected to unthinkable cruelty, she still believed "people are really good at heart." Robbed of freedom and future, she declared "I still believe, in spite of everything, that people are truly good at heart."

This is Anne's gift: not just a record of evil, but a testament to the beauty and resilience of the human spirit. Her story proves that even in the darkest circumstances, love and hope can flicker defiantly. Generations find in her words a light that cannot be extinguished, a voice that cannot be silenced, a heart that cannot stop hoping. In decoding her genius, we decode the best of ourselves.

Ten Quotes that capture the Heart of Anne Frank

Anne Frank's diary, "The Diary of a Young Girl," contains many memorable quotes that have resonated with readers around the world. It would be remiss if we did not include some of the most popular and impactful quotes from Anne Frank and our thoughts on how they display Anne's heart:

1. "How wonderful it is that nobody need wait a single moment before starting to improve the world." July 6, 1944.

   - This quote reflects Anne's optimistic outlook and her belief in the power of individual action.

2. "In spite of everything, I still believe that people are really good at heart." July 15, 1944.

   - Despite the horrors she witnessed, Anne maintained faith in the fundamental goodness of humanity.

3. "I don't think of all the misery, but of the beauty that still remains." March 7, 1944.

   - Anne's ability to focus on the positive aspects of life, even in dire circumstances, is evident in this quote.

4. "Whoever is happy will make others happy too." March 6, 1944.

- Anne understood the ripple effect of happiness and how it can spread to others.

5. "I can shake off everything as I write; my sorrows disappear, my courage is reborn." April 5, 1944.

- Writing served as a therapeutic outlet for Anne, helping her to cope with her fears and challenges.

6. "No one has ever become poor by giving." March 26, 1944.

- This quote speaks to the value of generosity and altruism.

7. "People can tell you to keep your mouth shut, but that doesn't stop you from having your own opinion." October 11, 1942

- Anne valued free thought and the importance of maintaining one's personal beliefs and opinions.

8. "Think of all the beauty still left around you and be happy." March 7, 1944.

- Anne's advice encourages focusing on the beauty in life despite hardships.

9. "Parents can only give good advice or put them on the right paths, but the final forming of a person's character lies in their own hands." July 15, 1944.

   - This quote highlights Anne's belief in personal responsibility and self-determination.

10. "Human greatness does not lie in wealth or power, but in character and goodness. People are just people, and all people have faults and shortcomings, but all of us are born with a basic goodness." July 6, 1944

   - Anne's perspective on true greatness and the inherent goodness in people.

These quotes reflect Anne Frank's wisdom, resilience, and hope, which continue to inspire and move readers worldwide.

Chapter 2: Timelines of Hope

Anne Frank's diary became one of the most poignant and influential books of the 20th century. It offered a deeply personal perspective on the Holocaust and inspired generations with its message of resilience and hope. To fully appreciate the impact of her words, we must understand the historical trajectory of her life and the publication journey of her diary. This timeline charts the critical milestones, from a private journal to a global symbol of the indomitable human spirit.

1929: Annelies Marie "Anne" Frank was born on June 12 in Frankfurt, Germany to Otto and Edith Frank.

1933-1934: As Adolf Hitler rose to power and anti-Semitism spread in Germany, the Frank family moved to Amsterdam, Netherlands, hoping to find safety.

1940-1942: In May 1940, Germany invaded and occupied the Netherlands. Anti-Jewish measures were enacted, forcing the Frank family into hiding. On June 12, 1942, Anne received a red-and-white plaid diary for her 13th birthday. She named it "Kitty" and began writing immediately. On July 6, 1942, the Franks moved into a secret annex at 263 Prinsengracht, joined later by four other Jews seeking refuge.

1942-1944: For two years, Anne chronicled her daily life, thoughts, and feelings while hiding. She wrote about the fear of discovery, the challenges of communal living, her budding romance with Peter van Pels, and her dreams and aspirations. Despite her circumstances, she maintained an unwavering belief in people's fundamental goodness.

1944: On August 4, after over two years in hiding, the residents were discovered and arrested by the Gestapo, likely due to a tip. They were sent to transit camps and then deported to Auschwitz. In October, Anne and Margot were transferred to Bergen-Belsen, where conditions were horrific.

1945: In February 1945, just weeks before liberation, Anne and Margot succumbed to typhus at Bergen-Belsen. Of the eight people from the Secret Annex, only Otto Frank survived the Holocaust. After the war, Miep Gies gave Otto Anne's saved diary.

1947: Otto Frank fulfilled Anne's wish by publishing her diary in Dutch as "Het Achterhuis" in an edition of 1,500 copies.

1950s: The diary was translated into German, French, and English. The English version "Anne Frank: The Diary of a Young Girl" became a bestseller. It was also adapted for stage and screen.

1960s: The Anne Frank House museum opened in 1960 and became a site of pilgrimage and education. The diary's authenticity was challenged, but proven by experts.

1990s-2010s: The diary continued to be translated into dozens of languages and incorporated into educational curricula as a teaching tool about the Holocaust and human rights. New editions and adaptations were released.

Present Day: Anne Frank's diary has now sold over 30 million copies in over 70 languages worldwide. Her story continues to resonate and inspire. The Anne Frank House remains vital for Holocaust education and promoting tolerance.

Anne's diary transcends tragedy to become an eternal voice of resilience, hope, and faith in humanity's fundamental goodness. This timeline underscores its extraordinary journey from a young girl's private words to a global phenomenon touching millions of lives. It's a testament to storytelling's enduring power and the indomitable human spirit.

Truth in the Pages

Anne Frank's diary powerfully testifies to the resilient human spirit. Her words, written while hiding from Nazis during World War II, reveal an honest and moving account of a young girl's innermost thoughts. Despite constant fear, deprivation, and witnessing human cruelty, Anne's writing brims with optimism, introspection, and hope.

On July 15, 1944, just weeks before her arrest, the 15-year-old Anne wrote, "It's a wonder I haven't abandoned all my ideals, they seem so absurd and impractical. Yet I cling to them because I still believe, in spite of everything, that people are truly good at heart." This unwavering faith defies her nightmarish circumstances. Her words don't express blind optimism but a profound capacity for empathy and philosophical depth, astonishing for one so young.

Anne grappled with complex questions of identity and existence. On April 11, 1944, she pondered, "Who has made us Jews different from all other people? Who has allowed us to suffer so terribly up until now? It is God that has made us as we are, but it will be God, too, who will raise us up again." Her musings reveal a resilient spirit seeking meaning amidst suffering.

Beyond her words, Anne's enduring impact testifies to her story's power. Published in 1947, her diary has sold over 30 million copies in over 70 languages. It has inspired films, plays, curriculum – and countless individuals across generations and cultures. Many cite Anne's words as key influences, shaping values, careers, and commitments to justice.

Miep Gies, who hid the Frank family and preserved Anne's diary, reflected: "Never a day goes by that I do not think of what happened then." Gies' words highlight how Anne's story inspires moral courage and compassion, reminding us of our shared humanity's imperative to resist oppression. Human rights groups harness Anne's tale to educate about the dangers of hate and promote diversity.

Ultimately, personal testimonies best reveal the diary's profound effect. "Reading Anne Frank's diary was life-changing," said one reader. "Her spirit, her belief in people's goodness despite suffering – it gave me perspective on challenges, inspired me to stand for what's right and never lose hope." Such reflections capture the book's lasting legacy.

Anne Frank's diary transcends being just a historical record. It vividly testifies to the human capacity for resilience, empathy, and hope amidst darkness. Her indelible words, echoing across decades, remind us of our shared humanity and potential for goodness.

In turbulent times, her voice shines as a beacon inspiring us to create a kinder world.

Legacies of Light

Anne Frank's story and words have left a profound impact on the world. They illuminate vital lessons about the human spirit, hope, and our shared humanity. Her diary stands as a powerful testament - one voice inspiring, educating, and transforming across generations. Here are some key legacies of light that Anne's life and writing have bestowed upon us:

First, Anne's story powerfully demonstrates the resilience of the human spirit in the face of unimaginable adversity. Despite constant fear, confinement, and deprivation, she maintained a remarkable capacity for joy, curiosity, and hope. She wrote, "I don't think of all the misery, but of the beauty that still remains." This ability to find light in darkness testifies to the strength within us all to persevere through challenges.

Second, Anne's unwavering optimism and hope, even in the bleakest times, stands as an inspiration. Her famous words, "I still believe, in spite of everything, that people are truly good at heart," show her extraordinary capacity to maintain faith in humanity. This hopeful outlook was a conscious choice, a defiant act of moral courage. Anne's example encourages us to nurture hope as a force for resilience and change.

Third, Anne's writing brims with profound empathy and a desire to understand others, even her persecutors. She grappled with complex moral questions, seeking to comprehend motivations behind actions. This capacity for empathy, to see the humanity in all people, is crucial for building a more compassionate world. Anne inspires us to strive for understanding, to bridge divides, and recognize our shared humanity.

Fourth, Anne's diary poignantly records her personal growth and self-reflection amidst extraordinary circumstances. She candidly explored her evolving identity, relationships, and beliefs. This introspective journey reminds us of self-reflection's importance for personal development and finding life's meaning.

Fifth, Anne's story has rallied people to stand against injustice and oppression. Her experience puts a human face on the Holocaust's horrors, making its lessons viscerally real. Countless individuals and organizations have drawn on her legacy to educate about discrimination, antisemitism, and dehumanization's dangers. Her voice continues inspiring commitment to a more just and equitable world celebrating diversity.

Sixth, Anne's diary poignantly expresses the universal human need for connection, love, and belonging. Despite isolation, she found solace in writing, dreams for the future, and relationships. She wrote, "I want to go on living even after my death." This desire to leave a mark, feel part of something greater, resonates across human experience. Anne's story reminds us to cherish connections, build community, and find belonging in challenging circumstances.

Finally, Anne's legacy powerfully demonstrates words' and storytelling's transformative potential. Her diary has touched millions, bridging cultures, generations, and experiences. It has inspired countless artistic works, becoming a conduit for empathy and understanding. This is one individual voice's power to create ripples of change, touch hearts and minds across time and space. Anne's example encourages harnessing our stories' power to create connection, understanding, and inspiration.

Anne Frank's diary is a luminous testament to the human spirit, offering enduring lessons about resilience, hope, empathy, personal growth, justice, connection, and storytelling's power. Her words and example continue guiding us, lighting the way toward a more compassionate, just, and humane world. As we navigate challenges and strive for positive change, we can draw strength and inspiration from Anne's unforgettable legacy of light. Her voice echoes across history, urging us never to forget our shared humanity and to always strive for a brighter future.

Chapter 3: Lessons from the Annex

Chronicles of Confinement: The Annex Timeline

To truly comprehend the extraordinary journey and challenges facing the Frank family, we must revisit the critical events that marked their years of confinement. The tale started on July 6, 1942, Otto, Edith, Margot, and Anne—left their ordinary lives behind. They moved into the concealed rooms above Otto's company at 263 Prinsengracht in Amsterdam. Soon after, Hermann and Auguste van Pels, their son Peter, and Fritz Pfeffer (a dentist and family friend) joined them. These eight individuals would spend the next two years hiding from the Nazi regime, their lives intertwined in a delicate dance of survival.

The early days were a flurry of activity as the inhabitants settled into their new reality. They blacked out the windows, arranged furniture to maximize space, and established rules for daily existence. Just 13 years old, Anne began documenting her experiences in a diary she received for her birthday. Little did she know that her words would become a testament to the resilience of the human spirit amidst unimaginable adversity.

As weeks turned into months, the Annex inhabitants fell into a routine punctuated by fear, boredom, and surprising lightheartedness. They spent days reading, studying, and engaging in quiet activities. Anne found solace in writing, pouring her heart onto the diary's pages. She wrote about her dreams, frustrations, and unwavering belief in people's goodness, even as the world outside descended into madness.

Confinement was not without challenges. Tensions ran high in the cramped quarters, with arguments and personality clashes erupting regularly. Food was scarce, and the constant fear of discovery weighed heavily. Yet, amid the hardships, moments of joy and celebration emerged. They observed birthdays and holidays, finding comfort in familiar rituals. Anne's irrepressible spirit often led the charge in creating games and distractions to lift everyone's moods.

In June 6, 1944 the Allied forces had landed in Normandy, signaling the beginning of the campaign to liberate Europe from Nazi control. Anne recounts there was a great commotion as they listened in to the announcement over the radio. She wrote "Hope is revivevd within us." Their elation was short-lived. On August 4, 1944 their worst fears were realized when German security police discovered the hidden entrance to the Annex. The eight residents were arrested and transported to Westerbork transit camp, their fates now in their captors' hands.

From Westerbork, the Annex inhabitants were deported to Auschwitz, the notorious Nazi concentration camp. Men and women were separated, with Hermann van Pels being gassed upon arrival. Edith and Margot succumbed to the harsh conditions and deprivations of the camp, perishing mere weeks before liberation. Anne, separated from her father, was sent to Bergen-Belsen, where she contracted typhus. She died, along with her sister Margot, in February 1945, just months shy of her 16th birthday.

Otto Frank was the sole survivor of the Annex group. After the war, he returned to Amsterdam, where he discovered Anne's diary, preserved by Miep Gies, one of the brave individuals who had helped hide the families. Recognizing the power of his daughter's words, Otto worked tirelessly to publish the diary, ensuring that Anne's voice and the story of the Annex would never be forgotten.

Today, the Secret Annex stands as a testament to the strength and resilience of the human spirit. It has become a pilgrimage site for millions, a tangible reminder of the Holocaust's horrors and the importance of standing against hatred and intolerance. Anne's diary, translated into over 70 languages, continues to inspire generations, offering a poignant glimpse into the heart and mind of a young girl whose unwavering belief in humanity's goodness shone bright even in the darkest times.

The Secret Annex's timeline is more than dates and events. It is a story of courage, hope, and unbreakable bonds of family and friendship. It reminds us of life's fragility and the importance of cherishing every moment. Most of all, it stands as a testament to the enduring power of the human spirit to find light in darkness, love in the face of hate, and hold onto hope when all seems lost.

Whispered Fears: What Were They Hiding From?

Imagine living every day in constant terror. You jump at every unexpected sound, fearing that any moment could bring discovery and doom. This haunting question lies at the heart of Anne Frank's story - the experience of hiding in the Secret Annex during the Holocaust with her family.

The danger of being found loomed large. Perpetual anxiety and claustrophobic confinement were inescapable realities as they sought to evade the Nazis' genocidal campaign. Whispered fears permeated every corner, every conversation, every waking thought. But what exactly were they hiding from?

On the surface, the answer seems obvious - they hid from the Nazis and their collaborators who rounded up and deported Jews to concentration camps. The Franks hid from Nazism's genocidal ideology that viewed Jews as subhuman, targeting them for extermination. They hid from the machinery of the Holocaust - the ghettos, cattle cars, gas chambers, and crematoria. The physical threat was clear and terrifyingly present.

But to fully grasp the psychological toll, we must look deeper. Their fears extended beyond physical dangers. They feared losing their humanity and dignity, as Nazi ideology sought to strip Jews of their basic human rights, reducing them to objects, numbers, and ultimately ashes. By hiding, Anne and her family fought to preserve their individuality and right to exist as equal human beings. They hid from dehumanization and degradation.

They also hid from the trauma of separation and loss. Going into hiding often meant leaving loved ones, friends, and communities behind. It meant severing ties with the outside world, living with constant uncertainty about the fate of those left behind. Anne wrote achingly about missing her friends, her school, her normal life. The fear of permanent separation haunted the inhabitants of the Annex.

Living in constant fear and anxiety took an immense mental and emotional toll. The stress of confinement, the never-ending vigilance, and the need for silence and stillness for hours corroded their psychological well-being. Anne wrote about tensions, conflicts, moments of despair and breakdown. They hid not just from external threats but from internal threats to their sanity.

Hiding also meant losing autonomy and control over their lives. The decision, while courageous, was a surrender - not to the enemy but a relinquishing of freedom and self-determination. They depended on their helpers for necessities and adapted to a regimented existence dictated by secrecy. They hid from the loss of their independence and agency.

On an existential level, they hid from the abyss of meaninglessness the Holocaust represented. The Nazis' campaign assaulted the value and sanctity of human life itself. By hiding, Anne and her family asserted the meaningfulness of their existence in the face of a regime that sought to negate it. They hid from a world where their lives were deemed worthless.

For those in hiding, these fears were visceral, immediate, and relentless. Fear was in the air they breathed, the silence they maintained, the darkness they retreated into. It was in every creak overhead, every knock at the door, every wailing siren.

Yet, remarkably, in the face of overwhelming fears, they found resilience, courage, and hope. They maintained humanity and dignity in undignified circumstances. They found solace in company, meals, and quiet conversations. They found purpose in bearing witness, documenting their experiences.

Anne's diary testifies to the human capacity to find light in darkness, nurture hope in despair. Her words remind us that even amidst unimaginable horrors, the human spirit can shine with radiance.

Reflecting on the Secret Annex's whispered fears challenges us to confront human cruelty and courage. We're reminded of the fragility of values like dignity, equality, freedom, and compassion - and the vigilance required to protect them.

Anne's story calls us to be guardians of these values, to stand against hate and dehumanization. It urges us to recognize humanity in every person, regardless of race, religion, or background. It challenges us to build a society celebrating diversity and upholding human rights as inviolable - a society where no one must live in hiding.

The whispered fears echo through time, but so too does the unwavering spirit of those who faced them. In honoring their story, we commit to the ongoing work of tolerance, justice, and human dignity - ensuring the light of hope triumphs over darkness.

A Day in the Annex: Unveiling the Unseen

It might seem a strange thing to ask you, but close your eyes for a moment and imagine spending even a day hidden with the others in the Annex. The quiet stillness of dawn settles over Amsterdam. While most people see the rising sun as the start of a new day filled with possibilities, for Anne Frank and seven others in the Secret Annex at 263 Prinsengracht, daylight brings only silence and constant fear of discovery.

The Secret Annex, a hidden apartment concealed behind a movable bookcase in Otto Frank's office building, has become their entire world. In this confined space, they must carefully measure and control every sound and movement. The most ordinary daily routines become survival rituals of profound significance.

Thrown together by the desperate need to escape Nazi persecution, these eight individuals must navigate living in forced intimacy while maintaining hope amidst growing despair.

The constant threat of discovery dictates every aspect of their lives. The Nazis relentlessly hunt Jews in hiding, and the consequences of being found are unimaginable. They must remain utterly quiet during the day when the office below is occupied. No running water, no flushing toilets, no creaking shoes on the floorboards. They are prisoners in their own hiding place.

To cope, they develop strict rules and routines. During the daytime silence, they read, study, and write - Anne faithfully records her experiences in her famous diary. In the evenings, they can move about more freely but with utmost caution.

Food, rationed and supplied by trusted Dutch friends risking their lives, is scarce but represents more than just nourishment. Mealtimes offer communion, a chance to gather and share not just food but stories, memories, and dreams of a better future.

Despite the constant stress and deprivation, moments of joy and normality still find their way in. Anne often instigates games and diversions to lift everyone's spirits. They celebrate holidays and birthdays, clinging to these rituals as reminders of their humanity.

But the outside world's specter is never far away. They listen intently to the radio, each Allied victory bringing hope, each setback plunging them into despair. They yearn for the day they can emerge from hiding and reclaim their lives, but grapple with the possibility that everything and everyone they once knew may be lost forever.

Their ability to maintain sanity and selfhood for two years of fear and confinement is a testament to human resilience. They support and care for each other, forming a makeshift family bonded by trauma and hope. And through Anne's diary, they leave an enduring legacy - a firsthand account of the Holocaust's harsh realities and a timeless message about the power of the human spirit to endure unimaginable adversity.

Yet their story's ending underscores the limitations of their efforts. Despite all precautions and sacrifices, they were betrayed and discovered in August 1944. All were arrested and deported to concentration camps.

This heartbreaking conclusion forces us to confront difficult questions. Could they have done anything differently? Were their efforts futile against such overwhelming evil? But it also highlights the importance of their resistance, however small or seemingly doomed. In hiding, they defied the Nazis' attempts to erase their humanity, surviving not just physically but spiritually while maintaining dignity, love, and hope amidst unparalleled darkness.

Their story provides an intimate view into the human cost of hatred and intolerance. Behind every statistic and historical fact are real individuals with dreams, fears, and an unquenchable will to live. It challenges us to examine our own capacity for good and evil, and to stand against injustice wherever we encounter it.

As we imagine a day in their lives, we are invited into a shared space of humanity. Their story transcends time and place, speaking to universal experiences of fear, hope, and love amidst adversity. It reminds us that even in the darkest times, the human spirit can endure and even flourish.

Light in the Dark: Finding Hope Within Walls

The cramped Secret Annex put immense strain on Anne Frank and the seven other Jewish refugees hiding there during World War II. They squeezed into small rooms, cut off from the outside world, constantly fearing discovery and deportation. Their physical confinement mirrored the suffocating reality of living under Nazi occupation, with their freedom severely limited by genocidal hatred. In this pressure cooker, maintaining hope might have seemed impossible.

Yet, Anne's diary and accounts from others reveal they found remarkable ways to nurture hope and affirm their humanity. Rather than despair, they courageously chose to live as fully as possible within constraints. They clung to the belief that goodness and beauty existed, even temporarily overshadowed by war's shadow and hatred.

Anne's diary stands as a profound testament to hope. She poured out dreams, fears, and insights with stunning honesty and wisdom beyond her years. Writing became her lifeline, helping her process experiences and envision a better future. "I can shake off everything as I write; my sorrows disappear, my courage is reborn," she confided. The simple act of writing each day courageously affirmed her voice and spirit could not be silenced.

Creative pursuits and learning helped Anne and the others transcend physical limits. They rigorously studied and wrote, determined to continue education and development. This commitment proclaimed the Nazi worldview would not define or limit them. By expanding minds, they asserted freedom and humanity in the one realm walls could not confine.

Shared bonds and daily rituals also gave them hope. Preparing meals, exchanging small gifts, playing games—ordinary routines took extraordinary meaning as acts of resistance and affirmation. Observing birthdays, religious holidays, and milestones proclaimed joy, faith, and human connection still mattered, even in darkness. Each small celebration was a candle against the enveloping gloom.

Movingly, they found hope in empathy and forgiveness. Living in close quarters inevitably caused conflicts. But as Anne matured, she responded with compassion, not judgment. "In spite of everything I still believe that people are really good at heart," she wrote, a staggering affirmation of faith in humanity despite having every reason for cynicism. Her capacity to hope for others' goodness, even those who wronged her, became her most profound resistance against a hate-filled ideology.

Ultimately, the fragile hope the Annex inhabitants created could not withstand the crushing force of Nazi occupation. Betrayed and arrested, most perished in concentration camps. Yet even in those darkest times, trapped in human cruelty's abyss, Anne and others found glimmers of hope. Survivors recount small kindnesses among prisoners—affirmations of goodness in extremis.

In one sense, the Annex story ends in heartbreak and defeat. But in a deeper sense, it stands as a victory for the human spirit against impossible odds. By daring to hope, to affirm beauty and meaning, Anne and her fellow refugees denied their oppressors' ultimate triumph. The Nazis could take lives, but not humanity or faith in life itself.

Their example calls us to nurture hope's flame in our own challenging times. We may not face the same extremes, but we all struggle to find light in darkness, whether personal or societal. Anne reminds us hope does not depend on external situations, but on our daily choice to affirm the good, the possible. Hope is a radical act of envisioning reality beyond present limits.

Cultivating hope is both individual and communal. Like Anne, we find it through creative expression, intellectual exploration, and cherished routines. But we also find it by reaching out, building empathy and solidarity. Each kind word, each small caring act, is a shared candle dispelling gloom.

Reflecting on Anne's story in our era of rising intolerance and existential threats, let us commit to keeping hope alive—not as passive wishing, but as defiant optimism. Let us honor her legacy by fiercely defending dignity, celebrating diversity, and asserting the power of arts and education to elevate spirits. Let us dare imagine a world where no child hides from hate, and work to realize that vision.

For in the end, the Secret Annex's message is not despair, but resilience. Anne and her fellow refugees showed the human spirit can nurture hope in hopeless circumstances, find beauty in squalor, and affirm love in hate's face. They call us to not just witness their story, but participate in its unfolding legacy, be keepers of the light they tended in darkness.

Life Lessons From the Annex: Keys to Courage and Hope

Anne Frank and her fellow inhabitants of the Secret Annex learned profound lessons during their years in hiding. The experiences chronicled in Anne's powerful diary offer deep insights into living with courage, hope, and grace despite unimaginable adversity. By examining these lessons, we can find inspiration and guidance to navigate our own challenges and live resilient, purposeful lives.

The first key lesson is the power of hope. Amidst the Holocaust's darkness, Anne held fast to hope. She wrote, "Where there's hope, there's life. It fills us with fresh courage and makes us strong again." Her words remind us that hope sustains us through the most challenging times. Anne's hope wasn't naive optimism - she faced grim realities head-on. Yet she chose to focus on the possibility of a better future, dreaming of becoming a writer, traveling, and seeing friends again. These dreams gave her a reason to keep going and find meaning in confinement.

The second lesson is finding beauty in the mundane. Confined to a small space, Anne and her companions could have succumbed to despair. Instead, they infused their days with beauty and wonder. Anne delighted in sunlight through the attic window and birds singing outside. She lost herself in books and poured her heart into her diary. This ability to appreciate small pleasures was more than a coping mechanism - it was a spiritual practice of staying present and grateful.

The third lesson is the importance of self-reflection and personal growth. Anne's diary was a tool for self-discovery. Through writing, she grappled with profound questions of identity, morality, and purpose. She declared, "I want to go on living even after my death! And therefore I am grateful to God for giving me this gift...of expressing all that is in me." Her introspection resisted dehumanization by asserting her individuality.

The fourth lesson is embracing love and connection. In the Annex's crucible, Anne forged deep bonds with her companions and discovered romance's rush. She poured love into her writing as a way to connect with future readers. Love was an act of defiance, a way to see humanity's goodness when inhumanity reigned.

The fifth lesson is standing up for beliefs. At just thirteen, Anne had a strong sense of justice. She questioned authority and named injustice, bearing witness to Nazi occupation's realities. Her courage reminds us of our responsibility to make our voices heard, even in difficult times.

Anne Frank's lessons transcend time and circumstance. Cultivating hope, finding beauty, embracing self-reflection and growth, prioritizing love and connection, standing up for beliefs - these keys unlock our courage and potential. As we face today's challenges, let us draw strength from Anne's example. Let us hold fast to ideals, nurture our inner lives, and show up for each other with love and compassion. By honoring her legacy, we contribute to realizing her dreams of peace, justice and human connection.

Chapter 4: Anne and Modern Media

Anne Frank's story, born from her heartfelt diary written while hiding in the secret annex, has transcended the pages to become a powerful narrative adapted into numerous films and television series. As Anne sat in the annex, every creak of the floor and whisper of a neighbor potentially spelling disaster, she could scarcely have envisioned that her words would one day resonate with millions of viewers across the globe. The adaptations of her story, in various languages and formats, underscore the profound impact of her experiences and the universal relevance of her message.

In each cinematic and televised retelling, the immense hardships faced by Anne and the entire Frank family are brought to life, offering audiences a poignant reminder of the devastating consequences of hatred and intolerance. These adaptations not only preserve Anne's legacy but also invite us to reflect deeply on the implications of our actions in the world today. As we watch her story unfold on screen, we are reminded of the importance of empathy, understanding, and the enduring human spirit amidst adversity.

Each portrayal, whether through a documentary lens or dramatic reenactment, aims to honor Anne's legacy and educate future generations about the horrors of the Holocaust. They serve as powerful tools for remembrance and reflection, ensuring that the lessons from Anne's life continue to inspire and provoke thought long after the credits roll.

Here are notable films and TV adaptations about Anne Frank, along with brief descriptions of each:

1. The Diary of Anne Frank (1959) - Directed by George Stevens, this American film is one of the most famous adaptations of Anne Frank's diary. It won three Academy Awards and is praised for its faithful representation of the original play and Anne's life in hiding.

2. Das Tagebuch der Anne Frank (1967) - This television film from the United States adapts Anne Frank's diary for the screen, focusing on her life in hiding during World War II.

3. The Diary of Anne Frank (1980) - Another American television adaptation, directed by Boris Sagal, this version brings Anne Frank's story to a TV audience with a focus on the intimate details of her diary.

4. The Attic: The Hiding of Anne Frank (1988) - A TV movie that explores the period when Anne Frank and her family were hiding in the secret annex, highlighting the risks taken by those who helped them.

5. Anne Frank Remembered (1995) - Directed by Jon Blair, this documentary film features interviews, archival footage, and readings from Anne's diary to paint a comprehensive picture of her life and legacy.

6. Anne no Nikki (1995) - A Japanese anime adaptation directed by Akinori Nagaoka, this film offers a unique animated portrayal of

Anne Frank's diary, bringing her story to an international audience in a different format.

7. Anne Frank: The Whole Story (2001) - This television miniseries directed by Robert Dornhelm provides an extensive look at Anne Frank's life, from her early years to her time in hiding and beyond. It includes dramatizations of events from her diary and historical context.

8. The Diary of Anne Frank (2009) - A BBC TV serial directed by Jon Jones, this adaptation offers a detailed portrayal of Anne's experiences, featuring a new script by Deborah Moggach. It aims to bring fresh perspectives on her diary.

9. Mi Ricordo Anna Frank (2009) - An Italian TV movie directed by Alberto Negrin, this film is based on the memoirs of Anne Frank's friend, Hanneli Goslar, and explores their friendship and experiences during the war.

10. Das Tagebuch der Anne Frank (2016) - A German film directed by Hans Steinbichler, this adaptation revisits Anne Frank's diary

with a contemporary perspective, emphasizing the emotional and historical significance of her writings.

11. Where Is Anne Frank (2021) - Directed by Ari Folman, this animated film reimagines Anne's story by following her imaginary friend, Kitty, who comes to life in present-day Amsterdam and embarks on a journey to find Anne Frank.

12. My Best Friend Anne Frank (2021) - A Dutch film directed by Ben Sombogaart, this adaptation focuses on the friendship between Anne Frank and Hanneli Goslar, providing insights into Anne's life from a friend's perspective.

13. A Small Light (2023) - A TV mini-series that tells the story of Miep Gies, the woman who helped hide Anne Frank and her family. It provides a broader context of the efforts made to protect Anne and the others in hiding.

These adaptations vary in format and perspective, offering different angles on Anne

Frank's life and the impact of her diary on the world.

Conclusion

Anne Frank's life, tragically cut short by the horrors of the Holocaust, continues to resonate deeply with people around the world. Born on June 12, 1929, in Frankfurt, Germany, Anne and her family moved to Amsterdam to escape Nazi persecution. However, as the Nazis occupied the Netherlands, the Franks were forced into hiding in the now-famous secret annex behind her father's business premises.

Anne Frank's story serves as a stark reminder of the atrocities of the Holocaust and the enduring spirit of those who suffered. Her diary has become a symbol of resilience and the importance of bearing witness to history. Through her eloquent and heartfelt writing, Anne Frank has left an indelible mark on the world, reminding us of the enduring strength of the human spirit in the face of unimaginable adversity

www.ingramcontent.com/pod-product-compliance
Lightning Source LLC
Chambersburg PA
CBHW051458140726
47987CB00006B/2762